SPOTTING DIFFERENCES

Llama
or
Alpaca?

by Christina Leaf

BELLWETHER MEDIA • MINNEAPOLIS, MN

Note to Librarians, Teachers, and Parents:

Blastoff! Readers are carefully developed by literacy experts and combine standards-based content with developmentally appropriate text.

Level 1 provides the most support through repetition of high-frequency words, light text, predictable sentence patterns, and strong visual support.

Level 2 offers early readers a bit more challenge through varied simple sentences, increased text load, and less repetition of high-frequency words.

Level 3 advances early-fluent readers toward fluency through increased text and concept load, less reliance on visuals, longer sentences, and more literary language.

Level 4 builds reading stamina by providing more text per page, increased use of punctuation, greater variation in sentence patterns, and increasingly challenging vocabulary.

Level 5 encourages children to move from "learning to read" to "reading to learn" by providing even more text, varied writing styles, and less familiar topics.

Whichever book is right for your reader, Blastoff! Readers are the perfect books to build confidence and encourage a love of reading that will last a lifetime!

This edition first published in 2020 by Bellwether Media, Inc.

No part of this publication may be reproduced in whole or in part without written permission of the publisher. For information regarding permission, write to Bellwether Media, Inc., Attention: Permissions Department, 6012 Blue Circle Drive, Minnetonka, MN 55343.

Library of Congress Cataloging-in-Publication Data

Names: Leaf, Christina, author.
Title: Llama or Alpaca? / by Christina Leaf.
Description: Minneapolis, MN : Bellwether Media, Inc., [2020] | Series: Blastoff! Readers: Spotting Differences | Audience: Age 5-8. | Audience: K to Grade 3. | Includes bibliographical references and index.
Identifiers: LCCN 2018055608 (print) | LCCN 2018056490 (ebook) | ISBN 9781618915757 (ebook) | ISBN 9781644870341 (hardcover : alk. paper)
Subjects: LCSH: Llamas--Juvenile literature. | Alpaca--Juvenile literature.
Classification: LCC QL737.U54 (ebook) | LCC QL737.U54 L43 2020 (print) | DDC 599.63/67--dc23
LC record available at https://lccn.loc.gov/2018055608

Editor: Al Albertson   Designer: Jeffrey Kollock

Printed in the United States of America, North Mankato, MN.

Table of Contents

Llamas and Alpacas

Llamas and alpacas
are fluffy **mammals**
with long necks.
Both are helpful
to people.

llama

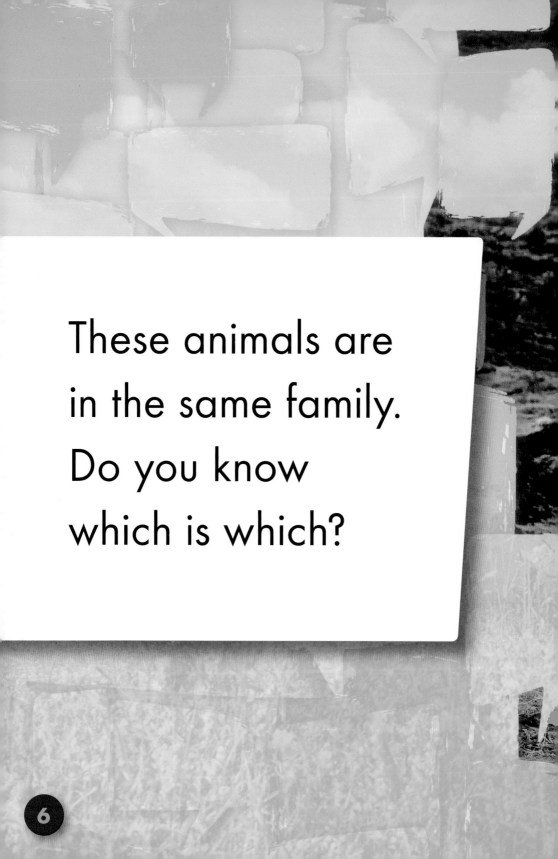

These animals are
in the same family.
Do you know
which is which?

alpaca

🔍 Different Looks

Heads show who is who. Alpaca faces are short and furry. Llamas have long faces.

Llama ears are tall and curved. Short, pointed ears belong to alpacas.

llama
ears

Alpaca fur is soft and fluffy. Llama fur is short and **rough**.

Llamas stand taller
than alpacas.
They can be 1 foot
(30.5 centimeters) taller!

Lifestyles set these animals apart, too. Alpacas hang with **herds**. Most llamas live alone.

alpaca herd

Both mammals help
people. Llamas carry
heavy **loads**.
Alpacas give soft **wool**.
Who are these helpers?

load

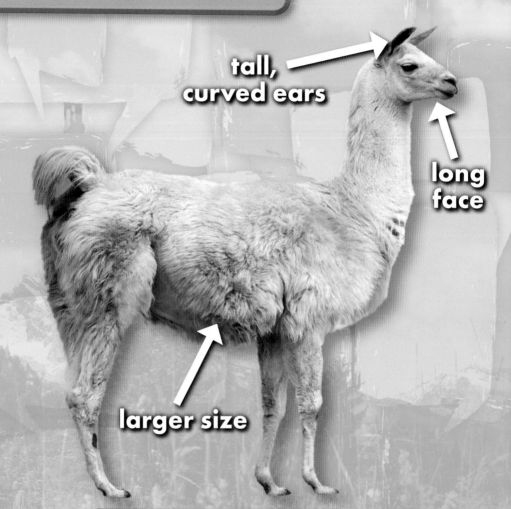

tall, curved ears

long face

larger size

Llama Differences

used as pack or guard animals

live alone

short,
pointed ears

smaller size

short,
furry face

Alpaca Differences

used for wool

live in herds

21

Glossary

herds

groups of animals

rough

not soft

loads

objects that are moved or lifted

wool

soft, curly hair or fur

mammals

warm-blooded animals that have hair and feed their young milk

To Learn More

AT THE LIBRARY

Bodden, Valerie. *Llamas.* Mankato, Minn.:
Creative Education, 2019.

Buxton, Jane. *The Littlest Llama.* New York,
N.Y.: Sterling, 2008.

Hasselius, Michelle. *Alpacas.* North Mankato,
Minn.: Capstone Press, 2017.

ON THE WEB

FACTSURFER

Factsurfer.com gives you
a safe, fun way to find
more information.

1. Go to www.factsurfer.com.

2. Enter "llama or alpaca" into the
   search box and click 🔍.

3. Select your book cover to see a list
   of related web sites.

Index

The images in this book are reproduced through the courtesy of: Cezary Wojtkowski, front cover (llama), whoever, front cover (alpaca); Thiago Bianchi, pp. 4-5; pickypalla, pp. 6-7; Galyna Andrushko, pp. 8-9; MrWildLife, p. 9 (bubble); Nyura, pp. 10-11; MayaCom, pp. 12-12; Marnix Foeken, pp. 14-15; Chris Wang, pp. 16-17; wanderluster, pp. 18-19; mariait, p. 20 (llama); Harald Toepfer, p. 20 (pack animal); Harry Zimmerman, p. 20 (alone); Eric Isselee, p. 21 (alpaca); J. Lekavicius, p. 21 (wool); Geoff Hardy, p. 21 (herds); Matyas Rehak, p. 22 (herds); Irina Mos, p. 22 (loads); Nadia Kompan, p. 22 (mammals); StockPassion, p. 22 (rough); bowron, p. 22 (wool).